Native
American
Peoples

INUIT

Michael Burgan

Gareth Stevens Publishing
A WORLD ALMANAC EDUCATION GROUP COMPANY

Please visit our web site at: www.garethstevens.com
For a free color catalog describing Gareth Stevens Publishing's list of high-quality books
and multimedia programs, call 1-800-542-2595 (USA) or 1-800-387-3178 (Canada).
Gareth Stevens Publishing's fax: (414) 332-3567.

Library of Congress Cataloging-in-Publication Data

Burgan, Michael.
    Inuit / by Michael Burgan.
        p. cm. — (Native American peoples)
    Includes bibliographical references and index.
    ISBN 0-8368-4219-7 (lib. bdg.)
        1. Inuit—History—Juvenile literature. 2. Inuit—Social life
and customs—Juvenile literature. I. Title. II. Series.
E99.E7B8895   2004
971.9004'9712—dc22   2004046690

First published in 2005 by
Gareth Stevens Publishing
A World Almanac Education Group Company
330 West Olive Street, Suite 100
Milwaukee, WI 53212 USA

Copyright © 2005 by Gareth Stevens Publishing.

Produced by Discovery Books
Project editor: Valerie J. Weber
Designer and page production: Sabine Beaupré
Photo researcher: Tom Humphrey
Native American consultant: Robert J. Conley, M.A., Former Director of Native American
    Studies at Morningside College and Montana State University
Maps: Stefan Chabluk
Gareth Stevens editorial direction: Mark Sachner
Gareth Stevens art direction: Tammy West
Gareth Stevens production: Jessica Morris

Photo credits: Native Stock: cover, pp. 4, 10 (bottom), 16, 18, 20 (top), 21; Corbis: pp. 6, 12, 13,
15 (top), 17 (both), 19, 20 (bottom), 22, 23, 24, 25, 26, 27; Peter Newark's American Pictures:
pp. 7, 9, 10 (top), 11, 15 (bottom).

Printed in the United States of America

1 2 3 4 5 6 7 8 9 09 08 07 06 05 04

Cover caption: Arctic Inuits have traditionally hunted using **harpoons**, such as the one this
man holds. A long piece of sealskin attaches the harpoon's sharp point to the wooden handle.

Contents

Words that appear in the glossary are printed in
boldface type the first time they appear in the text.

Origins

The People Called Inuit

The Inuits live in several countries that stretch across the Arctic, the world's cold, dry north. The Inuit homelands in North America include parts of Canada, Alaska, and the eastern and western coasts of Greenland. A small number of Inuits also live in a part of Russia called Siberia. The total Inuit population today is about 155,000.

Some Inuit groups have different names for themselves. The Native American people of Arctic Canada and West Greenland call themselves *Inuit*. Other names are *Inupiat*, *Yupik*, and *Inuvialut*. All these names mean "people" or "real people." In 1977, representatives from the various Inuit groups met in Alaska and decided they would use *Inuit* to describe all the different groups.

The Inuits wear jackets called **parkas**. Inuit parkas once had pointy hoods, supposedly so people could easily grab someone who fell through the ice into freezing water.

The Inuit Origin Story

No one knows for sure how the Inuits came to their homelands, but most of the Inuit groups tell a similar origin story. In the distant past, a young girl was forced to marry a man who was really a dog. When they had children, half were human and half were puppies. The mother put the puppies into one shoe and the children into another. The shoes turned into boats that carried their passengers to new homes. The children grew up to become the Inuits. The puppies sailed much farther away, and they became the white Europeans who later explored the Inuits' Arctic homelands.

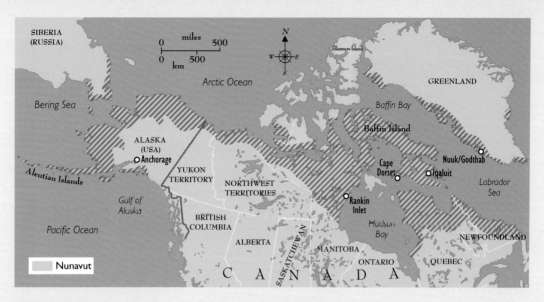

The orange area shows the Inuits' traditional lands. In some places, the Canadian territory of Nunavut, the Inuits' modern homeland indicated in yellow, overlaps their traditional lands. The cities and towns shown have large Inuit populations.

Scientists have a different way to explain how Inuits and other Native Americans first reached their homes: About twenty thousand years ago, some Asian peoples began moving eastward. Some may have sailed across the Pacific Ocean to Alaska or other areas in North America. Others probably crossed a landmass across the Bering Strait that may have once connected Siberia and Alaska.

The Language of the Inuits

There are several Inuit languages, but most speakers can usually understand each other. The following words are in Inuktitut, the language of the eastern Arctic:

Inuit	Pronunciation	English
li	ee	yes
aakka	ah-kah	no
qujannamiik	coo-yan-nah-mee-ick	thank you
liaali	ee-lah-lih	you're welcome
ikajunga	ick-a-yung-ga	help
tavvauvutit	tah-vow-voo-teet	goodbye

Chapter 2

History

The Arctic tundra is similar to a desert because it receives little rainfall each year and few plants can grow there. Just four hundred people live year-round on Canada's Ellesmere Island, shown here in late winter.

Early Arctic Dwellers

The first people to live in the Arctic **tundra** of North America are sometimes called Paleoeskimos. *Paleo* means "ancient," and *Eskimo* was the name European explorers gave the Inuits. The name came from an Algonquian Indian word referring to snowshoes — not to eating raw meat, as some people once thought.

The Paleoeskimos included the Dorset and Thule (TOO-lee) peoples. The Dorsets first appeared in northern Alaska about five thousand years ago. They then moved eastward into Canada and Greenland, living along the coast.

The Thules

About twelve hundred years ago, a new **culture** developed in Alaska. The people who created it are known today as the Thule people. The Thules were skillful sailors and hunters, tracking down sea mammals that lived far from the coast.

This photo from the late nineteenth or early twentieth century shows an Inuit husband and wife. In the past, Inuit parents sometimes chose their children's future spouses while they were infants.

Traveling mostly by water, the Thules followed the Dorsets eastward across North America, sailing through the many islands of northern Canada. No one knows why the Dorsets fled or died off as the Thules took over their lands. The Thules were the **ancestors** of today's Inuits in North America; their languages and culture come from the Thules.

Europeans and the Thules

In A.D. 985, a group of **Norse** settlers sailed from Iceland to Greenland. The Thules arrived in Greenland shortly after the Norse. By at least 1200, the Europeans and the Thules had discovered each other and began to trade goods. Over time, however, the Norse disappeared from Greenland, while the Thules spread out along the coast. Inuit tales say the Thules killed the Norse. Scientists think changes in the climate may have made it impossible for the Norse to survive in Greenland.

Following Food

The Thules most likely began to move out of Alaska searching for food. About A.D. 900, the temperature in the Arctic began to rise slowly. As the ice in Arctic waters began to melt, whales began moving eastward, and the Thules followed, because the whales provided most of the Thules' food.

The Age of Exploration

Starting in the fifteenth century, several European nations sent ships to explore the world. In the late sixteenth century, European sea captains thought they could sail through the Arctic Ocean and reach China. They called this supposed shortcut to Asia the Northwest Passage; their search for it led to the first contact between Europeans and the Inuits of Canada.

In 1576, English explorer Martin Frobisher reached Baffin Island in northern Canada while looking for the Northwest Passage. He met some Inuits and took one back with him to England. Hoping to start a colony in Canada, Frobisher returned the next year, but the ice and cold made life too difficult for the settlers who traveled with him. Over the next century, other Europeans continued to sail into Canada's Arctic region, looking for the Northwest Passage. Like Frobisher, they made limited contact with the Inuits.

Trading Goods

By the early eighteenth century, the French and British met more Inuits in Canada. From the west, Russians came to North America a little later, exploring and settling in Alaska. By the early nineteenth century, the Russians had made contact with the Inuits, after earlier dealing with the Aleuts, distant relatives of the Inuits.

The Europeans in Alaska and Canada sought animal furs and skins, which were used for clothing and fashionable beaver-skin hats. The French, British, and Russians all set up trading posts in remote areas and encouraged the Inuits to swap furs and skins for tools, guns, and other items. The Europeans also came to the Arctic to hunt whales. These sea mammals provided the oil used in lamps, whalebones used in women's clothing, and other materials. The sailors on the whaling ships also traded with the Inuits.

In this seventeenth-century painting, European explorers and Canadian Inuits battle. Few Europeans reached the center of the Canadian Arctic until the nineteenth century.

~~~ An Unexpected Trip ~~~

On his 1576 voyage to Baffin Island, Martin Frobisher captured an Inuit hunter. The English captain hoped the man could help him understand the Inuit language.

During Frobisher's second voyage, in 1577, the English battled the Inuits. After his men killed several Inuits, Frobisher took two more Inuits — a woman and her child — on board his ship. He then returned home with his captives. In England, the Inuit man demonstrated how he hunted with a spear and paddled his **kayak**. He and the other two Inuits died within a month of reaching England, probably from **pneumonia**.

These hunters would have eaten almost every part of the seal they just killed. The Inuits ate seal meat raw, boiled, frozen, and dried.

Changes in Inuit Life

In general, the Europeans lacked the Inuits' skills for surviving in the harsh Arctic climate. Through their trading posts and whaling ports, however, the Europeans influenced how the Inuits lived. More Inuits focused on the fur trade. With more frequent contact with Europeans, these Inuits began to rely more on European goods and less on traditional tools and ways of life.

The arrival of the Europeans also led to problems among the Inuits. During the nineteenth century, European diseases spread among the Inuits for the first time, killing many of them. Other Inuits developed **alcoholism** after the Europeans began trading them alcohol for their furs. Whalers killed so many whales that their numbers fell, threatening a key Inuit food source.

The Europeans also tried to change the Inuits' traditional religious beliefs. In Alaska, **missionaries** from the Russian Orthodox Church taught the Inuits the Christian religion. Protestant missionaries from England did the same in parts of Canada. Some Inuits accepted the Europeans'

Today, some Inuits in Alaska still go to Russian Orthodox churches. The word *orthodox* means "right belief."

10

faith. Others became Christian while still following some of their old religious traditions. The missionaries provided medical care for the Inuits and taught them European languages.

Arctic Exploration

Inuits played a key role for Europeans exploring the farthest reaches of the Arctic Circle. During one **expedition** in 1871, four Inuits helped European sailors survive a shipwreck off Greenland. The Inuits built **igloos** for the sailors and hunted for their food. Later explorers, such as Robert Edwin Peary, copied Inuit clothing, traveling methods, and hunting techniques and used the Inuits as guides. With Inuit help, Peary, an American, became one of the first people to reach the North Pole.

U.S. explorer Robert Edwin Peary reached the North Pole in 1909 with four Inuits. He began the trip with twenty-four men, nineteen sledges, and 130 dogs.

Travels with Peary

Although Robert Peary relied on the Inuits for help, he did not always treat them well. A Greenland Inuit named Minik Wallace described his experiences during a trip he and other Inuits took with Peary to New York in 1897:

We were crowded into the hold of the vessel and treated like dogs. Peary seldom came near us. When we reached the end of the sea voyage we were given the most miserable and unhealthy quarters on the steamship *Kite.* . . . [In] the Museum of Natural History in New York . . . we were quartered in a damp cellar most unfavourable to people from the dry air of the North. One after another we became ill and began to die off.

Later Inuit Life

During the twentieth century, Canada, the United States, and Denmark controlled the Arctic lands of North America. The governments of these countries promoted education and assimilation — the process of forcing the Inuits to accept U.S. and European culture.

In the past, most Inuits **migrated** between summer and winter hunting or fishing grounds. Under **Western** influence, they began to settle in permanent communities. By the 1960s and 1970s, more Inuits had indoor plumbing and electricity. Some Inuits also took on jobs at businesses set up by Canadian and U.S. companies. In Alaska, for example, the discovery of oil and the growth of the salmon fishing industry created jobs.

This Inuit village on Little Diomede Island, Alaska, was once a spring hunting site, but residents now live there year-round. In the local language, the village is called Inalik.

Political Activities

In 1924, the Inuits of Alaska became U.S. citizens. In 1959, Alaska became the forty-ninth state. Inuits and other Alaskans could now elect people to represent them in the U.S. Congress.

By that time, most Canadian Inuits lived in a region known as the Northwest Territories. For much of the twentieth century, only some Inuits within the Northwest Territories were represented in Parliament, Canada's lawmaking body. After 1962, the entire region elected a representative to Parliament. The Inuits also had more control over the laws within the Northwest Territories, and Inuits in other parts of Canada also played a larger role in running their own affairs. Starting in 1953, the Inuits of Greenland also won more freedom from the Danish government to control politics in their homeland.

Land Claims in Alaska

The law that made Alaska a state had a large impact on the Inuits. The U.S. government let the state of Alaska claim more than 100 million acres (40 million hectares) of land. The Inuits considered much of this land theirs. In 1966, a group called the Alaska Federation of Natives (AFN) began trying to reclaim this land for the Inuits and other Native Americans in the state. A 1971 U.S. law gave the Native Americans 44 million acres (17.8 million ha) of Alaska's land and almost $1 billion for other lands that they had lost.

In 1971, President Richard Nixon (second from right) met with Donald Wright (right) of the Alaska Federation of Natives to discuss land claims. The AFN represented Aleuts and Native Americans as well as the Inuits.

Traditional Way of Life

Different Ways of Life

Across the Arctic, the Inuits found ways to survive in a cold climate. During the winter, temperatures in some parts of the Arctic can drop below -40° Fahrenheit (-40° Celsius), and the Sun provides almost no light for months at a time. Farming there is impossible so the Inuits became expert at hunting and fishing. During the warmer weather of the brief Arctic summer, the Inuits' lives changed slightly. They could gather nuts, roots, and berries as well as hunt and fish. Because they settled across such a wide region, not all Inuits lived exactly the same way.

The Search for Food

During a typical year, most Inuits migrated from one area to another, searching for food. The Copper Inuits of central Canada, for example, hunted seals during the winter, searching for holes in the ice that the seals used to get air. Hunters waited for the seals at the holes, then speared them with **harpoons**. During the summer, the Copper Inuits moved onto land and fished or hunted caribou, musk ox, and other animals.

In other regions, such as Alaska, the Inuits sailed on small boats called umiaks to hunt for large sea mammals, such as walrus and whales, in the spring. Inuits across the Arctic also hunted in kayaks. Similar to canoes, these boats were built for just one person. Both umiaks and kayaks were made of wood and covered with animal skins. In general, most of the whale and walrus hunters also killed bear, fox, rabbit, and duck.

This photo from the early twentieth century shows Alaska Inuit hunters in their umiak. Modern umiaks use motors for power instead of sails and oars.

Inuit Housing

In Inuit, the word *iglu* means any kind of home, while the English word *igloo* refers to the famous Inuit snow house. Igloos were most common in the central Arctic, where other building materials were scarce during winter. Some Inuits lined the inside walls with sealskin to help keep their home warm. A hole in the upper wall let in light.

~~ Building an Igloo: An Hour's Work ~~

A nineteenth-century engraving of a typical igloo. The snow inside the igloo slowly melts and refreezes, creating a solid ice wall that makes the igloo sturdy.

Building an igloo took the right conditions and special skill. The snow had to be hard and deep so the builder could use his snow knife to cut large blocks that would not crumble. The builder, usually a man, worked from the inside of his igloo, taking the first blocks from what became part of the floor. When the outer walls were done, the builder's family used soft snow to fill in any gaps between the blocks. Inside, the mother smoothed out the floor and built a platform where the family would sleep.

An Inuit summer home, with a wooden frame and sod roof. In Alaska, the Inuits and their ancestors have used sod houses for thousands of years

In warmer months, some Inuits dug homes into small hills, adding wooden frames and covering the frames with rock or **sod**. Other Inuits used whalebone frames. Similar to tepees, tents made out of animal skins provided summer homes for some Inuits.

Social Life

The need to migrate meant the Inuits did not build large, permanent towns. Still, the Inuits usually had certain areas where they returned year after year. Several families would form groups called bands, and several bands united to form small communities. The families within a band or community might be related, but often two fathers formed a friendship that united their families. A family or band might decide to leave a certain community after a year or two.

The Inuits did not have formal governments or politics. The men of a community usually made decisions by debating an issue and coming to an agreement. In some regions, an older or very wealthy man might have more influence.

When food was scarce, the communities made sure that everyone received something from a successful hunt. The sharing was most common after killing a large sea mammal, with the largest portions going to the hunters. If food was available, the Inuits would not let someone starve.

These Nunavut Inuits prepare caribou for a local feast, carrying on the tradition of sharing food with all. Caribou remains an important source of food for many Inuits.

Family Life

The most important social unit was the nuclear family: a mother, father, and their children. Men hunted, built the homes, and made tools. Women prepared food, raised children, and made clothes from furs and skins, a prized skill since warm clothing was essential for surviving the winter. Women sometimes chewed sealskin to make it soft enough to sew. At times, women also helped fish and gather food for their families.

Most women tied their infants to their body under their large parkas to keep them warm. The babies often went naked, except for a diaper made of caribou skin. As children grew, they learned the skills they would need as adults. At times, they also had chores, such as gathering firewood.

A woman's parka had an oversized hood so it could easily hold an infant. A rope tied around the mother's waist kept the baby in place.

The Spirit World

According to traditional Inuit beliefs, the world is filled with spirits. Across the Arctic, the Inuits had different names and ideas about these spirits. In general, the spirits were invisible beings that filled the world. Sometimes they were ghosts of dead people or animals. The Inuits believed these spirits caused most of the illnesses, accidents, and other bad events that trouble humans. The Inuits feared the spirits and did not like to discuss them.

The Inuits also believed that humans had **souls**. Many Inuits thought animals had souls too, and some said everything in the world, including plants and rocks, had souls. The entire universe had a breath-soul commonly called Sila, associated with the air and weather.

While alive, a person had a breath-soul connected to Sila and a free-soul created by three goddesses — the Indweller in the Earth, the Sea Mother, and the Caribou Mother. Only the free-soul survived after a person died, usually traveling on to another world and then entering another human to live again.

The Shaman

At times, the Inuits needed to contact the spirit world, perhaps to end an illness or bring good weather. To communicate with the spirits, the Inuits relied on shamans, people thought to have special skills that would

Shamans wore masks like this during their religious ceremonies. Some masks represented spirits, while others might look like animals.

18

An Alaskan Inuit shaman tries to heal a sick boy in 1910. The Inuits believed their shamans could drive out evil spirits that caused sickness.

help them contact spirits. The shamans relied on ghosts or helpful spirits to do their work, and they performed ceremonies to talk with the spirit world.

The Inuits believed that shamans could perform miracles such as flying through the air or bringing the dead back to life. The shamans were the Inuits' doctors and sometimes their judges; a shaman might be asked to help settle a dispute. The Inuits also believed shamans could use their powers to curse people they disliked, sometimes leading to their death.

Using a hand drill, an artist makes holes in ivory. He spins the drill with a bow and uses a special tool in his mouth to keep the drill in place.

The Creative Inuits

The Inuits often revealed their artistic talents when they created the tools and other items they needed to survive. Women decorated clothing with leather, furs, and colorful beaded work. Men carved **ivory** decorations worn on clothing or as jewelry. Carvers also engraved images on larger bones or pieces of ivory. Shamans wore masks carved from wood or made of animal fur. Some Inuits in warmer regions made baskets out of coiled grass.

The Inuits also took time to sing, dance, and play music, often with animal-skin drums that looked like tambourines. They held dances to welcome visitors. During the winter, some communities built a large snow house that served as a dance hall. In summer, a large tent was used as the local social center. The Inuits danced and sang while musicians played.

Siberian Inuits in traditional clothes perform a dance. In their dances, the Inuits sometimes act out folktales or copy the movement of animals.

For centuries, the Inuits have enjoyed several kinds of wrestling. Both boys and girls compete in wrestling matches at the Arctic Winter Games, an event similar to the Olympics.

Fun and Games

Inuit social gatherings often featured games and sports, usually designed to test people's strength. Large groups sometimes took part in a tug-of-war, while two men might wrestle or have a punching duel. In this form of boxing, the men took turns hitting each other without trying to avoid their opponent's blows.

Another popular game was *ajagak*, which used a bone drilled with small holes. The bone was tied to a stick, and the player tossed the bone into the air and tried to get the stick into one of the holes. The Inuits also played a version of the fingers-and-string game known as cat's cradle to create animal shapes.

Child's Play

Inuit children had their own toys and games. Kids played hide-and-seek and a game called raven, similar to tag. One child was the hunter while the other players pretended to be ravens trying to escape the hunter. Children also played with dolls made from animal skins or carved from bones.

Chapter 4

Today

Old and New

Today, most Inuits blend their old customs with modern ways of life. They still go out on the tundra to hunt caribou and seal. Instead of riding on dog sledges, however, they speed across the ice and snow on snowmobiles. Planes provide contact with the outside world, transporting people and supplies. In Inuit towns, people drive **all-terrain vehicles.**

Small houses and log cabins have replaced the tents and sod homes of the past in villages and small towns. In some areas, the Inuits still build igloos as temporary homes while camping or hunting. Since sealskins dry out in heated houses, women in central Canada prefer to work with sealskins used for clothing in snow houses while actually living in framed wooden homes nearby. The Inuits wear the animal skins and furs along with modern clothing.

Snowmobiles are expensive to buy and run, but they help the Inuits travel across the tundra. Many Inuits use them for hunting.

Inuit Youth

Most Inuit children go to public schools, and some go onto colleges and universities, which are usually located in larger cities to the south. Over the past few decades, the Inuits have fought to make sure their schools teach students Inuit language and culture. Leaders do not want the students to become totally Western and forget their roots. At the same time, the children need to learn about the outside world if they plan to leave their small Arctic communities for larger towns. Television and other media have helped the Inuits learn more about the world beyond the tundra.

Inuit on Ice

In 2003, twenty-year-old Jordin Tootoo made history. Playing for the Nashville Predators, he became the first Inuit to reach the National Hockey League. Tootoo and his family reflect how the Inuits are combining the old and the new. His grandmother was born in an igloo in central Canada, and his uncle raises sled dogs, which are now used mostly for races. Tootoo learned to hunt seal with a harpoon, yet he easily surfs the Internet. With his professional hockey career, Tootoo has a chance to travel that few Inuits get. His goal is to one day bring the Stanley Cup, hockey's championship trophy, home to his village.

Jordin Tootoo (right) celebrates his first National Hockey League (NHL) goal.

The Inuits at Work

Many Inuits earn their income by traditional methods, such as trapping animals for their furs and fishing. In some areas, Inuits work in the mining or oil industries. Inuits also work in their communities as teachers, police officers, store clerks and managers, and government officials.

Some Inuits make their livings in the arts. Inuit artists sculpt, paint, and make prints, often showing scenes of Arctic life. Many mix modern techniques with traditional Inuit art forms. World famous for his work in stone, ivory, and other materials, Osuitok Ipeelee of Nunavut, the Inuits' modern homeland in Canada, began carving in the 1940s. His subjects include traditional Inuit images such as seals and caribou. Another well-known carver is Oviloo Tunnillie, a Nunavut Inuit who now spends her time in Ottawa and Montreal, Canada. Tunnillie comes from a family of artists. Her father Toonoo was one of the first successful Inuit sculptors.

Inuit writers, working in both Native and European languages, are reporters and novelists. Some write down ancient Inuit folktales, while others examine how the Inuits live in the modern world. In 2001, a group of Canadian Inuit filmmakers wrote and produced the first full-length movie ever made in an Inuit language, *Atanarjua (The Fast Runner)*.

An Inuit artist prepares to make a print. Some Inuit printmakers in Cape Dorset, Canada, cut an image into stone, apply ink to the image, then make their prints.

Traditional ways of life endure in Nunavut. Here, a fisherman catches Arctic char in a frozen lake.

Not all Inuits can make a living as they choose. In Alaska, whalers face limits on the number of bowhead whales they can kill. International groups worry that the bowheads will disappear, because so many of them have been killed over the centuries—mostly by nineteenth-century American and European whalers. The limits on whale hunting anger many Inuits, who argue that they should not be denied their traditional source of food because of the Western whale kills of years ago.

Hunting and fishing remains important to the Inuits because most food is expensive in the Arctic. Anything from outside the region must be brought on planes or ships. High transportation expenses make a gallon of milk cost about $10, while a quart of a soft drink might cost $8.

The Eskimo Scouts

Since Alaska came under U.S. control in 1867, some Inuits have worked for the U.S. military. During World War II, about six thousand Inuits, both men and women, watched for a possible enemy invasion; they were nicknamed the Eskimo Scouts. After the war, many of the Inuits joined the Alaska National Guard, and the old nickname endured. The Eskimo Scouts often trained U.S. soldiers, teaching them how to fight and survive in Arctic regions. Today, the Eskimo Scouts serve in the war on terrorism, watching for potential attacks against Alaska's oil pipelines, seaports, and airports.

A Nunavut mother and son stand next to a stone sculpture called an *inuksuk*. An inuksuk can be thousands of years old and might mark a path or warn of dangerous conditions.

Moving Forward

Over the last few decades, the Inuits have tried to make sure the governments that control their lands do not ignore them or take away their rights. In 2002, the Alaskan Inuits convinced an international whaling organization to raise the limit on the number of bowhead whales they could kill. The next year, the Thule Inuits of Greenland won a court case that required the Danish government to give them money for forcing them from their homes years before.

The different Inuit groups often work together to reach their goals. In 1977, the Inuits of Canada, Alaska, and Greenland formed the Inuit Circumpolar Conference (ICC). Inuits from Russia later joined the group. The ICC addresses issues that concern all Inuits. These include keeping pollution out of the Arctic, promoting traditional culture, creating Inuit-owned businesses, and guaranteeing the Inuits equal rights.

For thousands of years, the Inuits and their ancestors have lived in one of the most isolated regions of the world. They developed skills and knowledge that made life possible in a harsh climate. With the arrival of Europeans, the Inuit life changed forever. However, the Inuits have found a way to keep their traditions while adjusting to the demands of a different culture.

Nunavut

In 1999, the Canadian government turned a large portion of the Northwest Territories into a homeland for the Inuits called Nunavut ("our land"). About 29,000 people, mostly Inuits, live in this huge territory, which covers about 772,200 square miles (2 million square kilometers), an area larger than Alaska. Two Inuit languages are spoken here as well as Canada's two official languages, English and French. The territory has just twenty-six communities, and the capital, Iqaluit, has a population of about six thousand. Towns are isolated, with no roads connecting them. The people must fly or sail to travel across the territory. The creation of Nunavut gave the Inuits of the region more local political control than any other Inuits enjoy.

A winter scene in Iqaluit, the capital of Nunavut. Once called Frobisher Bay, the town used to host a U.S. military base. The largest community in Nunavut, Iqaluit is the smallest capital city in Canada.

Time Line

before 1000	The Thules, ancestors of the Inuits, begin to move out of northern Alaska and spread eastward along the Arctic Circle.
about 1200	The Thules make contact with the Norse in Greenland.
1577	Explorer Martin Frobisher takes three Baffin Island Inuits to England; all three died shortly afterward.
1700s	British and French explorers and traders make contact with Canadian Inuits.
early 1800s	A Russian fur company trades with Alaskan Inuits.
1840s	U.S. whaling ships begin operating off the Alaskan coast, severely reducing the whale population upon which the Inuits depend.
1867	The United States purchases Alaska from Russia.
1924	Alaskan Inuits become U.S. citizens.
1941–45	Inuit "Eskimo Scouts" in Alaska watch for possible enemy attacks during World War II.
1953	Greenland Inuits begin to win more local political freedom from Denmark.
1959	Alaska becomes the forty-ninth U.S. state, allowing Inuits to vote for representatives in the U.S. government.
1962	All Inuits of Canada's Northwest Territories are allowed to vote for a representative in Parliament.
1977	Inuits across the Arctic form the Inuit Circumpolar Conference to work on issues concerning all Inuits.
1999	Canada forms the territory of Nunavut, which is controlled by the region's Inuit population.
2002	Alaskan Inuit whalers win the right to kill more bowhead whales.
2003	Jordin Tootoo is the first Inuit to play in the National Hockey League.

Glossary

alcoholism: a disease in which people's desire to drink alcohol is so strong they cannot control it.

all-terrain vehicles: small, open, four-wheeled vehicles with large tires that can move easily over ice and snow.

ancestors: people from whom an individual or group is descended.

culture: the arts, beliefs, and customs that make up a people's way of life.

expedition: a trip taken for a specific reason, such as to explore an unknown area.

harpoons: spears with ropes attached so the throwers can pull their catch toward them.

igloos: dome-shaped dwellings built of blocks of hardened snow.

ivory: the long tusk, or tooth, of certain mammals such as a walrus.

kayak: a long, thin canoe usually built for one person.

migrated: moved from one area to another.

missionaries: people who try to teach others their religion.

Norse: describes people from northern Europe, particularly Norway, who settled in Iceland and Greenland.

parkas: warm fur jackets with a hood.

pneumonia: a serious illness making it difficult for a person to breathe.

sod: grass or turf.

souls: energies or invisible forces thought to create human life or be connected to gods; also the spiritual part of human beings.

tundra: a cold region with few or no trees and a layer of soil beneath the surface that always stays frozen.

Western: relating to European and North American culture.

More Resources

Web Sites:

http://www.kativik.qc.ca/ulluriaq/Nunavik/inuitlife Learn about Inuit life in Nunavik, Canada, including clothing, trade, tools, and a child's or teenager's day.

http://www.nunatinnit.net Check into this streaming media web site showing life on a remote outpost on Baffin Island. Includes text, movies, and photos.

http://collections.ic.gc.ca/arctic/inuit/people.htm Presents information on the history, land, economy, and traditions of the Inuit people.

Videos:

Atanarjua (The Fast Runner). Lot 47 Films, 2001.

My Inuit Family from Canada. Schlessinger Media, 2003.

Nanook of the North. Criterion Collection, 1998.

Books:

Bial, Raymond. *The Inuit* (Lifeways). Benchmark Books, 2001.

Corriveau, Danielle. *The Inuit of Canada* (First Peoples). Lerner Publications, 2001.

Finley, Carol. *Art of the Far North: Inuit Sculpture, Drawing, and Printmaking.* Lerner Publications, 1998.

Siska, Heather Smith. *People of the Ice: How the Inuit Lived* (How They Lived in Canada). Firefly Books, 1995.

Williams, Suzanne. *The Inuit* (Watts Library: Indians of the Americas). Franklin Watts, 2004.

Wolfson, Evelyn. *Inuit Mythology.* Enslow Publishing, 2001.

Things to Think About and Do

The Weather and You

Find out the average temperature for your state during the winter. How does this compare to the temperatures in the Arctic? Make a list of the ways the weather in your region affects what you do during the winter and summer.

Working Together

Think of a problem in your local community. Who could you work with to try to solve this problem? What people would you have to talk to change the current situation? Would it be more helpful to talk to political leaders, teachers, or other students? Discuss this with other students.

The Need for Nature

What is one animal or natural resource that is important to your community today? How do people use it? What would happen to the community if that resource suddenly disappeared? Write a paragraph with your thoughts.

Build an Igloo

Using sugar cubes, shreds of paper mixed with glue or paste, or other materials, build a model of an igloo. Design the interior and craft the tools of the Inuit hunters such as harpoons and sleds that may be inside or outside the igloo.

Index